Green Smoothie Recipes & other Healthy Smoothie recipes

Discover over 50 Easy Smoothie Recipes – breakfast smoothies, green smoothies, healthy smoothies, lunchtime smoothies, yogurt smoothies, special occasion treat smoothies and fruit smoothie recipes

C Elias

D1306799

Contents

Introduction

In this day and age where eating healthy has become so important, many people still find it hard to eat enough fruit and vegetables at the recommended amounts per day.

Even though they know it is good for them, many still prefer not to eat it! It can be very difficult starting a healthy lifestyle if you are used to high carbohydrate and fat fast food. But smoothies are now becoming the new 'fast food' and healthy smoothies will make sure you are getting the fruit and veg you really need.

Drinking fruit juice is fine but some of the manufacturers do add a lot of sugar. Try to keep the sugar intake low by making your own. All you need is a blender, or smoothie maker plus the suggested ingredients of fruit and veg in the recipes that follow. It is that simple. You can add whatever you like though such as protein powders and healthy supplements to make your smoothies as nutritious as you wish.

Here are a few smoothie benefits:

1. By choosing the right ingredients, a smoothie can be a great way to cleanse and detoxify your body. This can help your health generally, but can also be good for conditions like acne.

2. Smoothies give you a real energy boost, not a fake caffeine kick.

3. They are quick and easy to prepare and are very mobile -- you can take them with you in the care and drink them on your way to work or while you run errands.

4. Fruit is packed with goodness, but it can be a real chore to eat as much of it as we should. So by drinking our fruit in a smoothie, we can consume plenty, and do it quickly.

5. Kids really like them. It is a great way to give your kids nutritious fruits and vegetables that taste really good. Your kids probably won't even realize how nutritious they are - they will suck those smoothies down so fast.

Using Frozen Fruit

Many people find that freezing their fruit before using it in a smoothie is a great way to get a thicker, cooler smoothie than you get by just adding ice. If the fruit you plan to use is large, like watermelon, it may be best to chop it into smaller pieces before putting it in the freezer.

Freeze the fruit on a plate or piece of aluminum foil, so the pieces don't stick together, and then transfer them to a clean container in the freezer for later use.

Vegetables can also be used in smoothies and I have included a whole section on Green Smoothies!

A smoothie is perfect to replace a meal, as a healthy snack or as a quick meal for on the go. I have divided this book up into chapters describing various types of smoothies to make it easier to find the type you are looking for. **Green smoothies** deserve a full section of this book because of their fantastic health properties. I hope you enjoy them all and remember to experiment!

General notes on smoothie making

Not sure how to make the perfect smoothie? Read on. It is really quite easy. You will need a blender – get the fastest one you can, because green smoothies will need it very fast to break open the nutrients in vegetables for quicker absorption into your body.

Most smoothie lovers use a banana and then a couple of other kinds of fresh or frozen fruit. You can use peaches, mangos, strawberries, blueberries, raspberries, or any other kind of fruit you prefer. Be sure to pick up some low-fat or non-fat yogurt as well. Yogurt adds nutrition and is good for creating the creamy texture in smoothies. You can pick up protein powder or supplements as desired to add. To make a smoothie 'green' and sneak in some extra nutrition, just add a handful of green leafy vegetables!

When you have collected all of the ingredients you need, the fun can begin. It is time to make your smoothie. For more icy textures add a few ice cubes. When you have the smoothie blended just right, simply pour it into a glass and enjoy with a spoon or a straw.

I can suggest for those who have a sweet tooth – that you can add xylitol sugar. This is a polyol – a substitute for sugar that occurs naturally in the fibers of many fruits and vegetables. It is very low calorie, safe for diabetics with a very low glycemic index, has the same sweetness as sugar but won't spike your sugar levels. It is even anti-bacterial. You can read up on xylitol on the internet and see for yourself. But you should be able to purchase it online or at your local health food store. However don't give it to your pets – it does not agree with them and can make them very ill.

You can also use stevia powder or liquid which is a natural herbal sweetener and has no calories. In other words, no need to use unhealthy normal sugar anymore!

Milk:

You can use yogurt or milk in smoothies – obviously yogurt will give it a thicker texture. Natural organic yogurt with natural cultures of bacteria within it would be the best you can get – replenishing your intestines with good bacteria that will boost your immune system.

If you use cow's milk consider finding 'raw milk' – natural health experts now recommend you get raw milk rather than pasteurized and homogenized milk. The best milk is organic raw milk – from a source you know and trust.

Raw milk has all the nutrients and enzymes that have otherwise been removed from normal pasteurized milk. (see my book on **Healthy Eating Tips** at Amazon.com)

However, for many reasons people may prefer non cow's milk and you can use almond milk, oat milk, rice milk etc. as an alternative. Soy milk is used as well in smoothies but soy is now not considered a healthy substitute for cow's milk – the health risks appear to outweigh the advantages. The only soy variety one should be eating is the fermented soy bean. However, please research this yourself and decide!

Smoothies for kids

Even kids will love smoothies. It is a great way to get your kids to eat their fruits and begin to enjoy making healthy eating choices. Put their smoothies in fancy cups and allow them to make a party out of it. Smoothies will not have any artificial sweeteners, but the natural sugars in fruit make the smoothies seem as good as ice cream or desserts. Your kids should enjoy any of the recipes in this book with their favorite fruit and you can even sneak in some vegetables!

Smoothies versus energy drinks

We can see variety of energy drinks in cans or in bottles on TV commercials, in the market and even in local stores. Each of them are promoting and telling you about how it would increase your resistance, healthy performance and mind functions. Convincing you about its probable benefits, and its special characteristic that vary give them the edge among the other brand.

However, these Energy beverages are quite expensive and many are not safe to drink due because they contain artificial additives and high dosages of stimulants such as caffeine, which may cause worst effect on some people.

Why try to suffer the consequences of these products, when you can just make your own Homemade energy drink – The Smoothie! You will know exactly what goes in your Smoothie plus you can keep it natural and organic as well if you wish.

Fruit Smoothies

Apple Kiwi & Melon Delight Smoothie

Ingredients:

2 Cup honeydew melon, cut into pieces

2 kiwi, peeled and cut into pieces

1 green apple, peeled, cored and cut into pieces

1 TBSP lime juice

4 TBSP natural healthy xylitol sugar or stevia liquid

1 Cup ice cubes

Place all the fruit pieces into the blender.

Add the lime juice and blend 30 seconds to combine.

Sprinkle in the sugar and add the ice cubes.

Continue blending until mixture becomes very smooth.

If you prefer, you can leave out the natural sugar or stevia completely – your taste buds may not need any more sweetness!

Pear Smoothie

Ingredients:

1 Bart let pear, peeled, cored and cut into small chunks

½ Cup seedless grapes

1 banana, cut into small chunks

2 tsp. honey

¼ Cup cranberry juice (unsweetened)

6 ice cubes

Place the pears, grapes, banana and honey into the blender.

Puree until very smooth.

Add the cranberry juice and pulse 2 or 3 times until mixed together.
Add the ice and blend until mixture begins to thicken.

Kids love this smoothie. The fruit mixed with honey gives it a slightly sweet taste that appeals to children, or you can leave it out.

If cranberry juice doesn't suit your taste, try another juice.

Papaya Fruit Combo Smoothie

What You Need:

1 Cup orange juice (pure)

1 Cup papaya, peeled and diced

½ Cup cantaloupe, peeled and diced

½ Cup mango, peeled and diced

2 apricots, pitted and diced

Pour the orange juice into the blender.

Add the papaya, cantaloupe, mango and apricots.

On medium speed puree mixture for 1 minute.

Add some ice cubes for a cool drink.

Strawberry Crush Smoothie

Ingredients:

½ Cup unsweetened pineapple juice

¼ Cup unsweetened grapefruit juice

4 strawberries, stemmed and cut into pieces

1 banana, peeled and cut into pieces

Pour both juices into the blender.

Add the strawberry and banana pieces.

Blend until mixture is smooth and as thick as you like.

If the mixture isn't as thin as you would like add a little more pineapple, grapefruit juice or both.

Continue to blend until the mixture is to your liking.

Superjuice Cherry Smoothie

Ingredients:

2 Cups cherries fresh or frozen

1 banana, peeled and cut into pieces

1 Cup pure cherry juice

Place the frozen cherries, the banana pieces and the juice into the blender.

Blend until smooth.

Pour into glasses and top with cherries for decoration.

This is a wonderful healthy drink full of antioxidants – and cherries are being hailed as the new superfood so don't hold back on creating this one!

Dairy-Free Blueberry Smoothie

Ingredients:

2 Cups of Blueberries approx (test according to your taste)

1 Cup of White Cranberry Juice (unsweetened) or Pomegranate Juice (unsweetened)

A squeeze of lemon

Ice if you are using fresh Blueberries – or if frozen you will not really need the ice

Place all the ingredients in the blender and mix until smooth.

If you want a thicker smoothie try adding banana.

Tropical Milk Smoothie

Ingredients:

2 Cups of frozen strawberries

1 Can of pineapples unsweetened

1 banana

2 Cups of milk (preferably raw milk)

Put ingredients in blender. Whirl until smooth.

This makes for truly delicious smoothie – for added punch you can add whey protein powder.

Coconut Mango Smoothie

Ingredients:

2 peeled and stoned Mangoes

1 tin or carton of coconut milk

Just put the ingredients into the blender and whizz it!

Great for a quick fruit blast.

Peel & stone two mango. Add a tin of coconut milk. Whizz.

Energizing Smoothies

Peach and Almond Snack Smoothie

Ingredients:

1 Cup orange juice

1 Cup frozen peaches

1 frozen banana, cut into small chunks

2 TBSP toasted slivered almonds

Pour the juice into the blender. Carefully add the peaches and banana.

Add the almonds.

Blend until smooth.

Pecans also work well in this smoothie.

For a little different taste, use pineapple juice in place of the orange juice.

Strawberry Lift Smoothie

Ingredients:

¼ Cup crushed pineapple, drained

1 apricot, chopped

4 strawberries, trimmed and chopped

1 banana, chopped

1 ½ Cup water

1 TBSP powdered skim milk

1 TBSP protein powder

1 tsp. flax oil seed

Place all the fruit into the blender. Blend just slightly to combine.

Add the water, powdered milk, powdered protein and flax oil seed.

Blend until smooth.

The protein powder and flax oil seed are optional if you prefer to leave them out but they are added for extra energy.

Blueberry Pecan Smoothie

Ingredients:

1 frozen peach

10 frozen blueberries

1 (6 oz) container frozen low fat vanilla yogurt (no sugar) or plain yogurt plus vanilla bean flavoring drops

½ Cup skim milk

½ TBSP pecans, crushed

½ tsp. salt

¼ tsp. vanilla

Place the peach and blueberries into the blender.

Add the yogurt and pulse a couple of times to combine.

Add the milk, pecans and vanilla.

Sprinkle in the salt.

Blend until just smooth.

The salt is optional if you prefer to leave it out.

Pineapple Power Smoothie

Ingredients:

2 bananas, peeled and cut in chunks

2 peaches, peeled, pitted and cut in chunks

1 (8 oz) can crushed pineapple, (unsweetened)

1 C milk

Place all the ingredients into the blender in the order they are listed.

Blend until mixture is smooth.

Serve cold.

This smoothie is great for kids as an after school snack.

It gives them comfort after a long day at school and a little energy to finish out their day.

You can use fresh pineapple and extra pure pineapple juice for more sweetness.

Experiment with the quantities to suit your taste!

Winter Cold Smoothie

This delicious and healthy smoothie will boost your immune system and energy.

Ingredients:

1 ripe banana

16 ounces of frozen strawberries

12 ounces of fresh orange juice

1 TBSP of blackstrap molasses (for added iron nutrients),

or 1 TBSP of brewer's yeast (for added protein),

or 1 TBSP of flaxseed oil (for added Omega-3 acids),

or 1 TBSP of bee pollen (for added amino acids). You do not have to use these extra ingredients, but they will really add sustenance to the drink.

Cut up the banana into chunks.

Place the banana and the strawberries into the blender.

Include the orange juice in the blender.

Blend until the mixture is of smoothie consistency.

Insert a pinch of lemon juice if too sweet.

Best

Yogurt

Smoothies

Melon Berry yogurt Smoothie

Ingredients:

½ of a cantaloupe, peeled, seeded and chunked

1 Cup fresh raspberries

½ Cup yogurt

1 ½ TBSP xylitol sugar to taste or stevia liquid – experiment with either

Place the cantaloupe and raspberries in the blender.

Gently fold in the yogurt.

Sprinkle with the sugar.

Blend until smooth.

Lime & Fruit Low Fat Yogurt Smoothie

Ingredients:

¼ Cup orange juice

¼ Cup pineapple juice

¼ Cup grapefruit juice

¼ Cup lime juice

4 TBSP low fat plain yogurt

1 Cup ice

Pour all four juices into the blender.

Add the yogurt and ice.

Blend until smooth.

If the drink is too thick for you add some extra juice of your choice.

Add one tsp. at a time blending after each addition to reach the desired consistency.

Peachy Perfect Smoothie

Ingredients:

1 nectarine, pitted and chopped

1 (6 oz) container peach yogurt frozen – sugar free or natural yogurt plus a chopped and pitted peach

½ Cup Pine-Orange-Guava juice

½ Cup lemonade – unsweetened (you can find fizzy drinks in supermarkets that do all different sorts of drinks with no sweeteners or sugar. Find a naturally sweetened lemonade. If you can't find one you can make your own – with sparkling water, squeezed lemons to suit, xylitol sugar or liquid stevia for sweetness.

Place the nectarine and peach yogurt into the blender

Add the juice and lemonade.

Sprinkle in the sugar.

Blend on high until smooth.

Cocoa Banana Smoothie

Ingredients:

1 1/2 Cup of crushed ice

2 ripe bananas

1 TBSP of cocoa powder

1/2 Cup plain yogurt or milk (you can use lactose free milks as well – feel free to experiment!)

2 TBSP honey or add xylitol sugar or stevia liquid for sweetness

The ice should be crushed.

When the ice is crushed, place the other ingredients into the blender and blend them together.

Use the low to medium setting and blend all the ingredients for approximately 30 seconds.

After the 30 seconds are up, set the blender on high and blend it for another 30-45 seconds, or until the mixture is liquid.

Strawberry Cream Smoothie

Ingredients:

8-10 strawberries

2 bananas

5 ice cubes

1/2 Cup of natural yogurt

Xylitol sugar or stevia liquid for additional sweetness

1/3 Cup of milk (any type – almond, oat, coconut, rice milk)

1 teaspoon of vanilla extract

The bananas should be cut in half so that the blender can chop them easier.

Place the strawberries and bananas into the blender.

Place the yogurt on top of the strawberries and bananas, then the ice cubes should be on the top.

Blend the mixture until it is smooth.

You could replace the strawberries with blueberries as an alternative or even place a few blueberries on the smoothie for extra nutrition.

Mango Berry Smoothie

Ingredients:

2 Cups of fresh Mangos

1½ Cup of plain yogurt

½ Cup of mixed berries

1½ Cup of ice

Put the mangos into a blender.

Stir them until their are no clumps.

Add the yogurt and berries.

Stir it again, then add the ice and press grind.

Breakfast Smoothies

Apples and Oatmeal Breakfast Smoothie

Ingredients:

2 Cup low fat milk

1 apple, peeled, cored and diced

¼ Cup raisins

½ Cup instant oatmeal

1 TBSP creamy peanut butter (unsweetened)

Place the milk, apple pieces and raisins into the blender.

Add the oats and place the peanut butter on top.

Cover and blend well.

This makes a great breakfast drink for children. It tastes like an old fashion oatmeal cookie with a touch of peanut butter. The raisins are optional.

Almond Breakfast Smoothie

Ingredients:

½ Cup milk

½ Cup almonds

1 banana, peeled and sliced

1 TBSP honey

2 TBSP vanilla yogurt unsweetened or plain yogurt and you add a tsp. vanilla extract to suit

Pinch of nutmeg

4 ice cubes

Pour the milk into the blender.

Add the almonds, banana, honey, yogurt and extract.

Sprinkle in the nutmeg.

Add the ice cubes.

Blend on high until frothy.

Replace the banana with a peach and the vanilla extract with almond extract to make a slightly different taste. If you aren't partial to nutmeg try cinnamon instead.

Coffee Breakfast Smoothie

If you can't go without your coffee in the morning try this recipe and slowly move to organic non-chemically decaffeinated coffee and wean yourself off eventually and use only for treats!

Ingredients:

1 Cup brewed coffee, cold

1 banana, peeled and sliced

1 (6 oz) container vanilla yogurt unsweetened or plain yogurt with added vanilla extract

2 tsp. sugar

4 ice cubes

Pour the coffee into the blender.

Add the banana and the yogurt.

Sprinkle in the sugar.

Add the ice cubes.

Blend on high until smooth.

Fruity Breakfast Smoothie

Ingredients:

1 banana

1 orange sliced and unseeded

1/2 Cup natural plain yogurt

1 Cup of orange juice

6 ice cubes

Mix together the fruits, yogurt, and orange juice.

When the mixture is smooth, insert the ice cubes.

Blend until it is of smoothie texture.

Lunchtime Smoothies

Garden Salad Smoothie

Ingredients:

1 (8 oz) container plain yogurt

1 cucumber, peeled, seeded and chopped

1 tomato, chopped

1 stalk of celery, chopped

3 romaine lettuce leaves

1 TBSP onion, minced

6 ice cubes

Salt and pepper to taste

Place the yogurt into the blender.

Add all the vegetables.

Place the ice on top.

Puree until smooth.

Add salt and pepper to taste.

Blend slightly to mix in the seasoning. Try this smoothie to get those vegetables in a refreshing drink even on the run!

Sweet Potato Pie Smoothie

Ingredients:

2 sweet potatoes, cooked and cooled

1 banana, peeled and sliced

2 (8 oz) containers vanilla yogurt unsweetened or plain yogurt with vanilla extract added

1 Cup milk

1 tsp. Natural xylitol sugar or stevia liquid to suit taste

10 ice cubes

Put the sweet potatoes and bananas in the blender.

Add the yogurt.

Pour in the milk.

Add the sugar.

Place the ice cubes on top.

Blend until very smooth.

Quick Lunch Smoothie

Ingredients:

1/2 Cup of cucumbers, cut into small chunks

1/2 Cup of sliced carrots

1 Cup of tomato juice

1 Cup of ice

Slice the vegetables into pieces that will fit into the blender.

Put the pieces into the blender and grind them together.

Include the juice and ice, blending for 1 minute approximately.

Fruity Lunch Pack Smoothie

Ingredients:

1 Cup of chopped mango

1 Cup of plain yogurt plus vanilla extract or vanilla yogurt unsweetened

1 Cup of crushed ice

If you like it sweet choose a natural sweetener according to taste – xylitol sugar, stevia liquid – or a little of your favorite fruit juice

Add the mango, yogurt, ice, and sugar into the blender.

Mix the ingredients for approximately 30 seconds on the high setting.

Make certain the mixture is smooth.

Apple & Pear Diet Lunch Smoothie

For this delicious and weight reducing smoothie, you will need the following ingredients:

1/2 Cup of apples

1/2 Cup of pears

1 Cup of low fat plain yogurt.

1 Cup of non-fat milk – raw milk or coconut or almond

1 cup of ice

Slice fruits into any size and place into the blender.

Include other ingredients.

Combine ingredients in the blender for 45 seconds, and then check the consistency to see if it is what you want it to be.

Although all the smoothies in this book can be used when you are dieting, especially the green smoothies, this particular smoothie is very simple and quick, and provides some goodness to keep you from snacking on high carbs before your main meal.

On the Run Smoothies

On the run Smoothie ideas – 6 fast recipes

When you don't have time for a meal keep these ingredients handy, throw them into your blender, mix, taste and add a bit more of what you need for the taste you like!

- Strawberry Orange Smoothie – Made with fresh or frozen strawberries, orange juice and honey. A wonderful sun-kissed drink to help you wake up in the mornings.

- Classic Blueberry Smoothie – Made with fresh or frozen blueberries, frozen juice and yogurt. Blueberries have lots of antioxidants, so you can enjoy this knowing you're helping your body stay strong and healthy.

- Tropical Five Fruit Smoothie – Made with banana, kiwi, mango, papaya and orange juice. Escape to the tropics with this exotic blend of flavors. Mangoes are packed with vitamins. A great energy recipe smoothie.

- Berry Brainstorm Smoothie – Made with frozen strawberries, blueberries, raspberries, juice and yogurt. The official drink of superheroes and people who need extra brain power to accomplish amazing tasks. A great frozen fruit smoothie recipe.

- Creamsicle Smoothie – Made with fresh cantaloupe melon, orange juice, vanilla extract and honey. This yummy drink will remind you of the ice cream version you enjoyed on lazy summer days as a child.

- Pina Colada Smoothie – Made with pineapple, banana, coconut and milk. A tasty slimmed-down version of the popular alcoholic drink. Drink it as you get ready to go out for the evening!

Green Smoothies

What are Green Smoothies?

We all know that getting as much fruit as we can in our diet is extremely essential for good health. But let's be honest here, how many of us can actually manage to incorporate that much fruit in their diets? We also know that incorporating greens in our diet is absolutely essential. But how often do we get to bed of an evening and realize we haven't really had enough good food that day?

You might be able to make up a quick salad for dinner or grab a piece of fruit for breakfast but are you getting enough fruits and veggies in your diet? Are your children getting enough greens or are veggies the last thing your kids would willingly want to eat? If you think your diet is lacking in this department, you are not alone.

There is a fast and easy solution though for adults without an abundance of time and children who are on the picky side. It ensures that you get a daily dose of several fruits and veggies, including those all important greens, and the best part is that you probably won't even taste them. How in the world can that be possible? The solution is a delicious green smoothie!

You may have heard of green smoothies before. They seem to be gaining in popularity among busy adults and families with children. It is easy to see why. What could be easier than taking a couple handfuls of veggies and greens, like carrots and spinach, and adding some strawberries, banana, or apples and then blending it all together to make a delicious and healthy drink or meal? One blender full can provide a wonderful after school treat for several kids or it could serve as a complete breakfast for a working parent.

Kids especially love the color of green smoothies, which can very from deep to light green or even be dark red or orange depending on the ingredients. There are literally dozens of fruit/veggie combos you can try so that you never become bored and green smoothies are a great way to use up the produce from your fridge that may otherwise go bad.

These amazing drinks are your first step to a healthy, energetic and balanced lifestyle. If you get your tumbler of a green smoothie everyday in the morning, you know that you're all set to go for the rest of the day!

Green smoothies as mentioned above, blend in a mixture of

51

fruits and leafy green vegetables. These green vegetables are a storehouse of amino acids, iron, chlorophyll, vitamins, minerals and fiber. When consumed, these vegetables enhance digestion by aiding the production of enzymes.

About Chlorophyll:

You may be wondering what the fuss is about chlorophyll...? A molecule of chlorophyll closely resembles a molecule of human blood. And according to teachings of Dr. Ann Wigmore, consuming chlorophyll is like receiving a healthy blood transfusion. So by drinking two or three cups of green smoothies daily you will consume enough greens for the day to nourish your body, and all of the beneficial nutrients will be well assimilated very easily.

Will you enjoy the taste of veggie smoothies...?

It may surprise you to find that the fruit masks the taste of the greens and veggies and if you use a high speed blender you will not see any sign of them in the smoothie either.

If your smoothie is not sweet enough for your liking, you can add a bit more fruit. Bananas for instance, are an excellent addition for a sweet and fruity smoothie. You get all the vitamins and nutrition from the all the healthiest foods without having to "taste" the ones you don't like.

For an extra nutrition boost you can add supplements such as wheatgrass powder, hemp protein, greens powder, chia seeds, or ground flax. Instead of adding plain water to your smoothies you can mix things up by adding fresh squeezed juice, club soda, or almond milk.

Green smoothie enthusiasts claim that they lose weight, have clearer skin, and have more energy than ever before. Green smoothies are a miracle in a blender.

Where did the Green Smoothie come from?

Green Smoothies were originally devised by Victoria Boutenko, who being a raw diet practitioner became interested in the benefits of consuming a large amount of fresh, green, leafy vegetables. She studied chimpanzees to figure out how, in spite of having about 99.4% similarities in their DNA structure as humans provided high resistance to deadly disease like cancer, Aids and various other heart diseases.

She found out that the standard American Diet consisted of only about 3% green vegetables as compared to a whopping 39% of the chimps diet. This had to be the answer. So Victoria tried to figure out various recipes by means of which she could include these items into her daily diet, hence the birth of the green smoothie!

I hope you enjoy your green smoothies and experience good health and energy. Remember to take time to experiment and when you have a favorite – mark it down. I have left a blank page at the end of this book for you to write your notes!

Why Blend the Greens?

We know that these leafy green vegetables are a great source of nutrients. But to get the full benefit of these nutrients, we need to chew the leaves for a long period of time. Plus, since our jaws aren't strong enough, we never really manage to extract all the nutrients. Moreover, digesting these leaves is also a problem because humans do not have a high enough acid content in their stomachs.

Blending takes care of these problems as the leaves are ground and the cells, containing the nutrients are completely ruptured. Therefore we get the full benefit of the amazing amount of nutrients present in these greens.

Green smoothies are therefore an extremely potent source of nutrients in a simple drink. Besides getting the nutrients from the leafy vegetables you are also getting nutrients from the fruit too! They taste great and boost your health – why wouldn't you learn how to make a few!

Green Smoothies and Overall Health Benefit

The health benefits of green smoothies are too many to be counted! Green smoothies aid your bodily functions and provide an amazing amount of nutrients to us.

Who would think that just one little glass of this drink could do so much for our body? This drink tastes so great as well that it beats off competition from sodas and cappuccinos!

Green Smoothies – A Wonder Food:

I've mentioned the amazing dose of nutrients in Green Smoothies but you can also add in that these greens are rich in fiber, which as we all know aids the functioning of the digestive system. They also dictate colon ecology and effectively eliminate waste.

Since they are rich in chlorophyll they have numerous health benefits - chlorophyll helps to purify human blood, get rid of bad breath and body odor and even cures anemia.

Antioxidants and phytochemicals present in the vegetables leave you feeling rich and energized throughout the day. Moreover, green smoothies do something else that is wonderful. They bring down the acidic pH of the human body into the alkaline range.

Did you know that cancer and most other diseases flourish in the acid pH range?

As most of us know, prevention is better than cure. So get a regular daily schedule going of green smoothies!

What greens do I use in green smoothies?

Spinach

Kale

Swiss Chard leaves

Collard Greens

Parsley

Dandelion Greens

Beet Greens

Turnip Greens

Romaine Lettuce

Green & Red Lettuce

Mustard Greens

Arugula or Rocket lettuce

Many people also like to add Wheatgrass to their smoothies. Wheatgrass has a high chlorophyll content that causes increased Haemoglobin production in the body which increases the oxygen carrying capabilities of the blood. The increased capability of the blood to carry oxygen has a number of health benefits including purification of the blood, improving blood sugar disorders, helping combat toxins such as carbon monoxide and other traffic pollutants, cigarette smoke and heavy metals that can get into the blood.

Other reported benefits include:

Improved digestion

Reducing blood pressure

Improved ability of the body to heal wounds

Chlorophyll found in wheatgrass can prevent the growth of harmful bacteria.

Helping prevent tooth decay

Has anti-ageing abilities and can keep the hair from greying

The Best Ways to Add Green Smoothies to Get a Healthy Diet

Green Smoothies are a wonderful way of beginning the day. Getting your tumbler of this amazing drink first thing in the morning is the biggest favor you can do for yourself. They leave you feeling fresh and energized throughout the day and who doesn't want to feel like they're ready for action throughout the day?

But Green Smoothies can be had anytime, as a snack, along with lunch, dinner etc. It is not essential that you have it for breakfast and breakfast only.

Green smoothies can be an accompaniment for other meals or a delicious snack. If you've just come back from work and you're feeling hungry, go in for a green smoothie. It fills you up and rejuvenates your tired body. You'll be all set to play with your dog or running around with your kids once you've had your fill of these amazing drinks!

To receive all the amazing benefits of green smoothies just make sure you have a combination of fruit and green, leafy vegetables.

Green Smoothies are made from a combination of 60% organic fruits and about 40% green vegetables.

Drinking green smoothies on a regular basis has also become popular with people looking to lose weight and gain healthy, glowing skin.

Creamy Green Smoothie Tip

If your kids crave a creamy smoothie, with a rich texture and mouth-feel, all you need to do is make a green smoothie with mangoes or bananas. Incorporate either of these two fruits into your smoothie and you will have the creamiest drink ever!

Your smoothie might even solidify and acquire a pudding-like consistency if you use bananas so you could make a green smoothie dessert too.

How to get kids to have Green Smoothies

At the initial stages, when you are introducing your family to the concept of a green smoothie, people might not be so receptive.

After all, greens are generally not on most people's list of favorite foods. Well, to trick your children into having these smoothies, just use baby spinach! It hardly has any taste and they will definitely not be able to tell whether you've put in spinach or not and will be asking for more and more and more!

Later on of course, you can experiment with your greens and try different recipes!

Try to add sesame seeds, raw flaxseed, or sunflower or even pumpkin seeds into your smoothies. These add even more fiber to the drink and hence make it even healthier.

What Are the Best Blenders for Green Smoothies?

One must be very careful while picking a blender for the purpose of making a green smoothie. This is because if you do not use a high speed blender, all the cells of the leafy green veggies will not be ruptured and the important nutrients will not be released from the cell.

Currently two blenders – the VitaMix and the Blendtec blenders seem to be the best. But shop around and see what you can find.

Tips on preparing a Raw Green Smoothie

Now you may want to know what kind of green veggies to include in your green smoothie - any kind of leafy green vegetables will do. Moreover, it is highly recommended that you rotate the green vegetables you use in the smoothies.

If you just start out, spinach is a good option. This is because spinach hardly has any taste and is virtually undetectable in the smoothie. So for all those of you who cringe at the thought of a "green" colored smoothie, this is the veggie for you!

Summary of procedure:

All you have to do after you've got your fruit and leafy green vegetables ready is put them all in your blender (preferably high speed), add sufficient water to the ingredients, so as to completely submerge them and then blend away. After you're done preparing your smoothie, then taste about one teaspoon of the mixture and try to figure out whether you want it more sweet, or more watery with a lower percentage of greens or more energizing with a higher quantity of greens.

If you want it sweeter, all you have to do is add more ripe fruit.

If you want the mixture to be watery, all you have to do is add a bit of water. If, however you want it to be a more energizing mixture, you need to add both water and green vegetables to it. Make the necessary modifications, according to your taste and just like that, your perfect raw green smoothie is ready to serve!

Can Green Smoothies Aid to Weight Loss?

Do green smoothies make you lose weight? This is one of the most frequently asked questions in the world of nutrition.

Of course if you replace a meal a day with a green smoothie and eat another 2 meals a day that are healthy and nutritious – cutting out as many carbs as you can and making more use of the carbs in vegetables, then you will lose weight.

I recommend you get my **'Healthy Eating Tips to lose weight naturally'** book on Amazon.com which explains the good foods you can eat, the bad foods to avoid, and gives you a shopping list to get you started.

Are Bananas a Good Choice in Green Smoothies?

Bananas are one of the most frequently used ingredients for green smoothies. But it has an extremely high glycemic index. Most people will be hesitant about incorporating bananas into their diet on a regular basis. But one must keep in mind that fruits with high glycemic index are discriminated against because most people subsist on a diet which is full of refined carbohydrates and sugars.

Fresh bananas are rich in enzymes, vitamins, fiber and minerals, along with of course the sugar. But this is very different from the calories which are found in refined carbohydrate products because they do not provide you with these other amazing benefits!

Of course, if you find that banana doesn't agree with you, try recipes for Green Smoothies which do not include bananas. You can experience good weight loss with the help of green smoothies, along with glowing skin and radically increased energy levels. Remember, a greener diet, is a cleaner diet! But your other meals must be healthy!

Green Smoothie Recipes

Banana-Kale Green Smoothie

Please note! You can add natural yogurt, greek yogurt etc to these recipes for thicker, creamier taste. Alternatively, use a fruit smoothie recipe and add a handful of spinach or kale!

Ingredients:

2 Bananas – 2

1 Cup of frozen Blueberries

2 TBSP Hulled Hemp Seed

2½ Cups of Water

5 Kale leaves

Put all the ingredients for the smoothie into a high speed blender and blend well.

Make sure all the ingredients are completely covered with the water.

You can also add crushed ice to the blender mixture to make yourself a chilled smoothie!

Berryblast Green Smoothie

Ingredients:

1 Cup of Blueberries

1 Cup of Raspberries

3 handfuls of Baby spinach

1 Apple

2 Cups of water

Put in all the ingredients except baby spinach into a high speed blender, making sure that all the ingredients are well-covered with water.

Blend the mixture for about 30 seconds until it reaches uniform consistency throughout.

Then add the baby spinach and resume blending until completely broken down into a smooth drink.

Ginger Green Smoothie

Ingredients:

1 inch of fresh ginger

1 Cup of Pineapple

1 large Mango

Half a head of Romaine lettuce

Put in all the ingredients apart from the lettuce, into a high speed blender and blend for about half a minute.

Then add the romaine lettuce and blend until a thick, smooth consistency is reached.

Dandelion and Apple Green Smoothie

Ingredients:

1 peeled Lemon

1 bunch of Dandelion greens

2 large Apples

1 large Banana

2 TBSP of Flaxseed

Water – Enough to cover ingredients

Put in all the ingredients into a high speed blender along with enough water to cover all the ingredients.

Banana is added to impart a creamy texture to the drink.

Blend until a uniform consistency is attained throughout!

Pear and Arugula Lettuce Green Smoothie

Ingredients:

2 or 3 Pears

1 Banana

2 to 2 TBSP of Hulled hempseed

1 bag of frozen Raspberries

Small bunch of Arugula lettuce (called Rocket as well)

Water – Around 2.5 cups

Liquid Stevia – For taste

Put all the ingredients into a high-speed blender and make sure that all the ingredients are covered with water.

Blend until a thick, creamy consistency is obtained. Your nutritious smoothie is ready!

Vegetable Boost Green Smoothie

Ingredients:

2 Cup vegetable juice

½ Cup carrot juice

1 tsp. hot sauce

1 tsp. lemon juice

4 spinach leaves

1 tsp. parsley flakes

12 ice cubes

Pour the vegetable juice and carrot juice into the blender.

Add the hot sauce and lemon juice

Place the spinach leaves into the juices.

Sprinkle in the parsley.

Carefully add the ice cubes.

Blend until mixture is creamy.

Simple Sweet and Green Smoothie

Ingredients:

1 handful of Parsley

1 Banana (frozen)

A couple ice cubes

Water

Mix all ingredients in a blender until smooth.

This is a very fast, no fuss smoothie.

Makes one serving.

Orange Essence Green Smoothie

Ingredients:

2 large Swiss chard leaves (ribs cut away)

2 whole oranges (no seeds but pith is okay)

Zest of an orange

1 banana (frozen)

Ice cubes

Water

Very simply mix all ingredients in a blender until smooth.

Makes a fresh breakfast!

Cool Blueberry Breeze Green Smoothie

Ingredients:

2 Handfuls of Chard

1 Cucumber

1 Cup of Strawberries

1 Cup of Blueberries

1 Banana

Mix all ingredients in a blender until smooth.

This smoothie is perfect for a summer lunchtime.

Chocolatta Green Smoothie

Ingredients:

1 banana

2 white peaches

2 handfuls spinach

2 tsp cacao

1 tsp Maca

Water.

Mix all ingredients in a blender.

This smoothie is great for an energizing breakfast.

Maca:

Maca is a root from Peru. It looks like a little turnip or radish, and is a traditional staple food in Peru. Maca is a very densely nutritious food that contains high amounts of vitamins, minerals, enzymes and all the essential amino acids.

Melon and Strawberries Green Smoothie

Ingredients:

2 Cup spinach or collard greens

1 ½ Cantaloupe (ripe and fresh)

4-5 large Strawberries

1 Cup of Orange juice

1-2 teaspoons lemon juice

Water – pour in a little at a time to get the liquid consistency you like.

Mix all ingredients in a blender until smooth.

Pineapple Paradise Green Smoothie

Ingredients:

1 Cup of frozen pineapple, chopped

2-3 large Kale leaves

1 ripe banana

2 fresh mint leaves

2 cups water

Mix all ingredients in a blender until smooth.

Popeye Green Power Smoothie

Ingredients:

2 Cups of spinach leaves or collard greens

1 stalk celery

1 ripe banana

1 Cup of frozen strawberries

1 Cup of frozen pineapple

Water

Combine all ingredients and mix until smooth.

Peach Power Green Smoothie

Ingredients:

2 cups spinach

1 cup fresh Cantaloupe, cut in chunks

1/4 cup frozen pineapple chunks

1/2 cup frozen peaches

1/2 cup orange juice

Water

Blend all ingredients together until smooth.

This smoothie has a very fresh, tropical taste.

Perfect for breakfast or a hot summer day!

Healthy Special Treat Smoothies

Pancake Day Smoothie Treat

Ingredients:

1 banana, cut into chunks

4 strawberries, stemmed and cut into chunks

8 oz. milk

1 TBSP almond butter – preferably organic & raw

2 tsp. maple syrup

Place the banana and strawberry chunks into the blender.

Slowly pour in the milk.

Add the almond butter and maple syrup. You can try this with honey, stevia liquid, xylitol etc as well to keep it healthy.

Blend until very smooth.

Try other types of fruit for a little change.

Peanut and Banana Chocolate Smoothie

Ingredients:

1 Cup chocolate milk, very cold

> (make your own with pure organic cocoa powder a little hot water and milk. Add natural sugar xylitol for sweetness or honey or stevia liquid – experiment with the different ingredients to suit your taste)

1 banana, peeled and cut into pieces

2 TBSP creamy peanut butter (unsweetened)

2 ice cubes, crushed

Place the milk into the blender.

Add the banana and peanut butter.

Carefully place the crushed ice into the blender.

Blend until smooth.

Drink immediately.

The Special Occasion Jammy Treat Smoothie

Ingredients:

1 Cup unsweetened vanilla yogurt or plain yogurt with added vanilla extract

1 banana, peeled and sliced

2 TBSP naturally sweetened strawberry jam

1 TBSP honey optional

Place the yogurt into the blender.

Add the banana and strawberry jam.

Pour in the honey.

Blend mixture on high for about 30 seconds.

Mixture should be frothy when ready to serve.

Conclusion

Get a good blender and start out with simple smoothies until you get confident in adding different fruits and leafy vegetables. And pass the word around about the benefits you experience as a smoothie drinker!

Notes: